DATE DUE

JUL 1 7 2010			

B.F. Jones Memorial Library
Aliquippa, Pennsylvania
724-375-2900

Before leaving library report all damage in books you are borrowing. Each borrower is held responsible for all books drawn on his card and all fines accruing on same.

Ten cents a day is charged for each book kept overtime. No new cards will be issued until all fines are paid.

DEMCO

THE WORLD OF
SPORTS

Paula S. Wallace

Gareth Stevens Publishing
A WORLD ALMANAC EDUCATION GROUP COMPANY

Please visit our web site at: www.garethstevens.com
For a free color catalog describing Gareth Stevens Publishing's list of high-quality books
and multimedia programs, call 1-800-542-2595 (USA) or 1-800-387-3178 (Canada).
Gareth Stevens Publishing's fax: (414) 332-3567.

Library of Congress Cataloging-in-Publication Data

Wallace, Paula S.
    The world of sports / by Paula S. Wallace.
        p. cm. — (Life around the world)
    Summary: Describes some of the most popular sports and games that are played in such countries
around the world as Australia, Brazil, Egypt, Germany, Japan, Russia, and the United States.
    Includes bibliographical references and index.
    ISBN 0-8368-3662-6 (lib. bdg.)
    1. Sports—Juvenile literature. 2. Games—Juvenile literature. [1. Sports. 2. Games.] I. Title.
GV705.4.W35 2003
796—dc21   2002036653

First published in 2003 by
Gareth Stevens Publishing
A World Almanac Education Group Company
330 West Olive Street, Suite 100
Milwaukee, Wisconsin 53212 USA

Produced by Design Press, a division of the Savannah College of Art and Design.
Designers: Janice Shay, Maria Angela Rojas, Andrea Messina.
Editors/Researchers: Gwen Strauss, Nancy Axelrad, Lisa Bahlinger,
 Susan Smits, Cameron Spencer, Elizabeth Hudson-Goff.

Gymnastics consultation courtesy of Coachwayne.com

Gareth Stevens editor: JoAnn Early Macken
Gareth Stevens designer: Tammy Gruenewald

Photo Credits
Corbis: /Wolfgang Kaehler, cover, page 11; /Richard Powers, page 23; /Danny Lehman, page 30;
 /Tom & Dee Ann McCarthy, cover, page 43.
Getty Images: /PhotoDisc, page 6; /Christoph Wilhelm, cover, page 7; /Eyewire, page 14;
 /Wayne Eastep, page 15; /Scott Markewitz, page 19; /Jay Freis, page 27; /Andre Gallant, page 28;
 /Peter Hince, cover, page 35; /Gary John Norman, page 39; /Benn & Esther Mitchell, page 42.
Picture Quest: /Stockbyte, page 12; /Image Ideas, Inc., page 34.
SuperStock: cover, page 31.
Additional photography by Campus Photography, Savannah College of Art and Design.

Illustration Credits
Hui-Mei Pan: pages 9, 10, 13, 18, 20, 21, 22, 24, 25, 26, 28, 29, 32, 36, 37, 38, 40, 41, 44, 45.

Printed in the United States of America

1 2 3 4 5 6 7 8 9 07 06 05 04 03

CONTENTS

Words that appear in the glossary are printed in
boldface type the first time they occur in the text.

All over the world, people play sports and games. What are your favorites? Do you like running and chasing? Throwing and catching? In this book, you'll learn about the many ways children play around the world. In South Africa, some games help children practice the important job of watching their family's cattle. In Russia, children play winter sports that take advantage of the cold climate. In Australia, children play with boomerangs, which have been part of their culture for thousands of years.

The game that is played by the most children in the greatest number of places throughout the world is soccer. Boys and girls play soccer not only on grassy fields but also in streets, on sidewalks, in parking lots, and even on basketball courts. Three thousand years ago, the first soccer balls were made out of chopped-up sea sponges tied together with cloth. Even today, balls can be made out of many things, such as socks tied together or balled-up leaves, string, or tape.

Playing together teaches children how to live together. Through sports, they can build friendships and understanding and learn how to work out their differences. Children who play together learn that having fun is more important than winning or losing. In every country, every day, children start their games with the same words — "Let's play!"

AUSTRALIA

Australia's national **mascot** is a boxing kangaroo.

Australians have raced camels, goats, cockroaches, and even earthworms!

Australians love the ocean. Their country has ten thousand different beaches along 22,000 miles (35,400 kilometers) of coastline as well as the world's largest **barrier reef**. It's no wonder that many of the most popular Australian sports, including swimming, sailing, sailboarding, and surfing, take place in the water.

Australian **Aborigines** (ab-uh-RIJ-uh-nees) invented the boomerang. A boomerang is a stick that is shaped like a wide V. When it is thrown, it hovers and turns in midair, gliding back to the thrower's hands.

Thousands of years ago, boomerangs were used for hunting birds. Today, boomerangs are used in competitions. Throwers compete in events such as the "Aussie Round." In this event, a thrower is judged on the distance his or her boomerang travels, the **accuracy** of its return, and the thrower's ability to catch it.

Surfing

Surfing is one of the main water sports in Australia. Surfboards come in all shapes and sizes. They sometimes have funny names, such as "the swizzle" and "the fat penguin." In Australia, young surfers often start out on smaller, flat bodyboards.

How to make a **Boomerang**

This boomerang is shaped like an X instead of a V. To have fun with your friends, make your own boomerangs, throw them, and see whose goes the farthest. Find an open space away from other people. Hold your boomerang vertically, or pointing up, by one of its blades so that the curved tips bend toward you. Raise your arm and throw the boomerang with a quick snap of your wrist. You may have to adjust the folds to get the boomerang to work just right. Give it a whirl!

You will need:
- pen or pencil
- cardboard that is at least
  2 x 9 inches (5 x 23 centimeters)
- ruler
- scissors
- stapler
- markers

1 To make the blades, draw two long rectangles on the cardboard. Each rectangle should be 1 x 9 inches (2.5 x 23 cm).

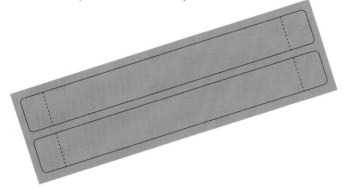

2 Cut out the blades. You can round the corners if you want to.

3 Lay one blade on top of the other in the shape of an X. Staple the blades together at the center.

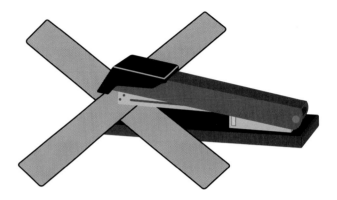

4 Decorate the boomerang with markers.

5 Fold the ends of each blade upward about 1 inch (2.5 cm).

BRAZIL

Did You Know?

Pélé (PAY-lay), the world-famous soccer player, dedicated his one-thousandth goal to the children of Brazil.

Brazilians are crazy about soccer. Maracana Stadium in Rio de Janeiro (REE-oh day zjah-NAIR-oh) is the world's largest soccer stadium. It was built to hold more than 200,000 spectators, and it is often filled when the most popular soccer clubs are playing in the city.

The biggest soccer matches are the ones for the World Cup, which is an international soccer tournament held every four years. Brazilians have great national pride in their World Cup teams. And no wonder — Brazil is the only country that has won the World Cup five times!

Brazil attracts many tourists to its beautiful beaches along 6,000 miles (9,650 km) of coastline. The beaches are also sports playgrounds for local children. Beach volleyball, surfing, sailing, and water skiing are very popular sports.

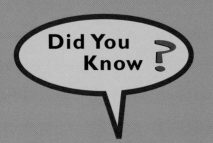

Secret Dance of Brazil

Capoeira (kah-poh-AY-dah) is a **martial art** of African origin that involves difficult gymnastic moves used in fighting and self-defense. Because African slaves in Brazil were forbidden to fight, they disguised the capoeira training to make the moves look like a dance.

How to play **Queimada**

Queimada (kee-MAH-jah) means "forest fire" in Portuguese, the national language of Brazil. The object of the game is to "burn" the players on the other team.

You will need:
- **six or more players**
- **large rubber ball, about the size of a soccer ball**

1 Divide the players into two teams. Mark off a place at each end of the playing area for a "cemetery." Each team chooses one player to stand in the cemetery. That player is "burned."

2 A burned player throws the ball to a teammate. That person catches it and throws it, as hard as possible, to a player on the other team.

3 If the player from the other team drops the ball instead of catching it, that player is burned and must go to his or her team's cemetery.

4 If the player from the other team catches the ball, he or she is not burned. The player with the ball can then try to burn players on the other team, either by running after them and tagging them or by throwing the ball to them as hard as he or she can.

5 Players in the cemetery can burn other players by getting the ball and throwing it, but burned players cannot leave their cemetery.

6 When all the players on one team are burned, the other team wins.

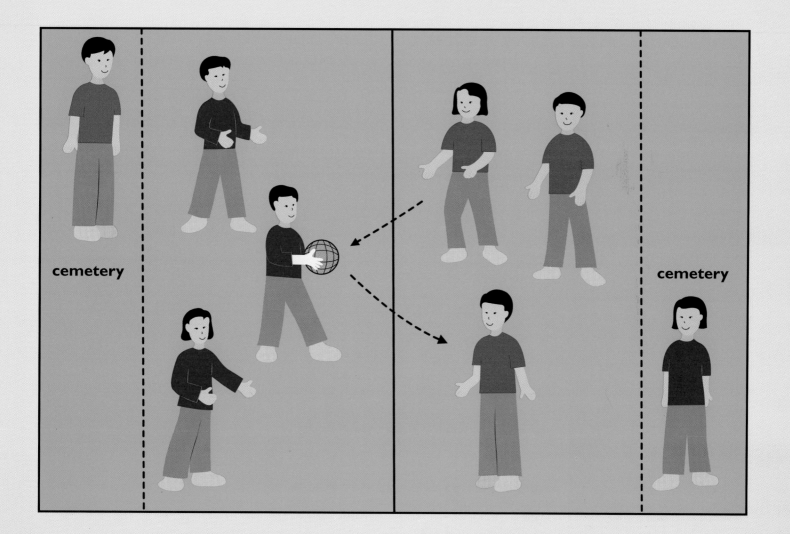

EGYPT

Did You Know ?

In the Egyptian town of Al-Arish, **Bedouins** (BED-oh-wins) gather each year for camel races. Bedouins are **nomads** who live in Egypt's Nile Valley.

Egypt was once divided into two kingdoms, the red kingdom and the white kingdom. After the two kingdoms were united, the **pharaoh** wore a double crown that was red and white.

Many of the sports that are played today were first played by the ancient Egyptians. Ancient **hieroglyphics** show scenes of both men and women involved in physical activities such as gymnastics, wrestling, weight lifting, rowing, swimming, and ball games. Boards for games such as *seega*, an ancient form of tic-tac-toe, have been found carved in stone in Egyptian tombs.

Ancient Egyptians made soccer balls out of pigs' bladders, pigskin, wound-up animal **sinew**, or chopped sea sponges wrapped in string and cloth. Linen balls have been discovered in Egyptian tombs. Today, Egyptian children play soccer whenever and wherever they can. In every street, alley, and vacant lot, children who want to play form teams. They might mark the goals with footstools or even piles of clothing. They may play one-on-one or share a **goalie** — anything to get a game going!

Ancient Cats

Egyptians were the first people to train cats to be household pets. Cats were admired and even worshiped as **deities** for their beauty, self-reliance, hunting skills, and cleanliness. The penalty for killing a cat in ancient Egypt was death!

How to play **Seega**

This ancient Egyptian game is a lot like tic-tac-toe. The object of the game is to put all three game pieces in a line, either horizontally or vertically, but not diagonally.

You will need:
- **two players**
- **six stones or small objects, divided into two sets**
- **tic-tac-toe board, drawn on paper or in sand, with three rows of three squares each**

❶ Players line up their stones on each side of the board in rows facing each other, leaving the middle row empty.

❷ Players take turns moving one stone per turn. A player can move any stone to any open square next to it.

❸ A player must move each of his or her stones at least once before he or she can win.

How to play the
Pyramid Bowling Game

In Egypt, children play this game with piles of bricks. They divide into a red team and a white team, like the two ancient kingdoms of Egypt before they were united by the pharaoh.

You will need:
- **two or more players**
- **blocks**
- **small rubber ball**

❶ Stack the blocks in the shape of a pyramid.

❷ Players take turns throwing the ball, trying to knock one block off the pyramid. When a player succeeds, he or she keeps the block that was knocked off and takes another turn. If a player knocks off more than one block, he or she must put the blocks back on the pyramid.

❸ When the whole pyramid is knocked down, the player with the most blocks is the winner.

17

GERMANY

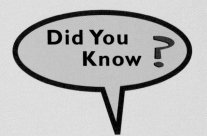

Did You Know?

In 1936, German boxer Max Schmeling beat famous American boxer Joe Louis in a match that was called "the upset of the century." Schmeling was the **underdog**.

Soccer is the most popular sport in Germany. The German national team is considered one of the top teams in the world. The West German soccer team won the World Cup three times.

Germans enjoy both indoor and outdoor sports. Swimming is a popular indoor activity. Every town has a public swimming pool, or *schwimmenbad* (SHVIM-in-bahd). Outdoors, children take advantage of Germany's mountains by hiking and rock climbing. During the winter, skiing is very popular.

Because there are no sports during school hours, most children participate in sports clubs after school. In fact, one out of every three German children and adults belongs to a sports club. There are clubs for handball, basketball, volleyball, tennis, swimming, cycling, rock climbing, hiking, and other sports. Children also enjoy playing traditional games of tag, such as *plumpsack*.

Olympic Games

Along with many other countries, Germany competes in the Olympic Games every four years. The modern Olympic Games, which started in 1896, are a revival of an ancient Greek tradition. Germany has won many gold medals in winter Olympic events, such as speed skating, downhill skiing, and **luge**.

How to play **Plumpsack**

There are no winners or losers in this game,
and you can keep playing for as long as you like.

You will need:
- **five or more players**
- **handkerchief**

1 The players sit on the ground
in a circle and choose one player
to be the plumpsack.

2 The plumpsack holds the
handkerchief and walks around the
circle behind the other players.

3 The other players sing,
"Don't turn around.
The plumpsack's going 'round.
If you turn around or laugh,
It will hit you on the back."

4 The plumpsack drops the
handkerchief behind a player.

5 The player must pick up
the handkerchief, chase the
plumpsack around the circle,
and tag the plumpsack before
the plumpsack takes the player's
empty space.

6 If the player
doesn't notice that
the plumpsack
dropped the
handkerchief, and
the plumpsack runs
around the whole
circle, the player
must sit in the
middle of the circle,
and the other players
say, "One, two,
three, lazybones!"
The lazybones is
freed when another
player is sent to
the middle.

7 If the player chases the plumpsack with the handkerchief and catches the plumpsack, the plumpsack must sit in the middle and be the "lazybones."

8 The player who chases the plumpsack always becomes the new plumpsack.

INDIA

Did You Know ?

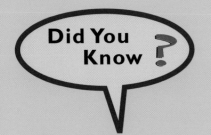

Yoga (YOH-guh) is a type of exercise that is over three thousand years old. In India, children learn yoga by imitating animals. Famous yoga poses have names such as "dog" and "cobra."

India's most popular sport is cricket. It was introduced to the country by the English when India was a **colony** of Great Britain. National teams compete at formal test matches, or cricket tournaments, which can last five days. Indian boys play a simpler form of cricket after school.

In rural areas, girls and boys often play sports separately. Many combine work with fun when they can. Girls often play singing games to entertain themselves while they work.

Kabaddi (kah-BAH-dee) is a sport that combines features of wrestling and rugby. It is called different names in different parts of India and is also played in other Asian countries, such as Pakistan, Nepal, Sri Lanka, Bangladesh, and Japan. No one knows the exact origin of this game, but it is believed to be about four thousand years old.

Kite Flying

Kite flying is a competitive sport in India. People spend years perfecting their flying techniques. The most fiercely played games involve kite fights, called *pacha* (PAH-shah). The object is to fly a kite so that it cuts the strings of the other kites in the sky. People use strings called *manjha* (MAHN-jah), which are **cured** with ground glass and glue to be very sharp.

How to play **Kabaddi**

In India, kabaddi is played in two halves. Each half is twenty minutes long with a five-minute break in between. The teams switch sides between halves.

You will need:

- **six to twenty players**
- **rope or chalk to mark a line between the two sides**
- **playing area, about 42 x 33 feet (13 x 10 meters)**
- **coin**

❶ Divide the playing area into two equal halves by drawing a chalk line or laying down a rope.

❷ Divide the players into two teams. Each team lines up about 20 feet (6 m) from the center line of the playing area.

"Kabaddi, kabaddi, kabaddi kabaddi."

❸ Toss a coin to decide which team starts the play. These players are the raiders.

❹ The raiders send one player to the other side. He or she chants "kabaddi, kabaddi, kabaddi," without taking a breath, while trying to tag the other team's players. A player who is tagged is out of the game.

❺ If the raider runs out of breath or stops saying "kabaddi" before getting back to his or her team's side, players from the other team can tag the raider out.

❻ A raider who is tagged is out of the game. A raider who returns to his or her team's side without being tagged keeps playing.

❼ The teams take turns sending raiders to the other side.

❽ The game ends when one team has no players left.

Another way to play kabaddi is to score one point for each player who is tagged. Players who are tagged then stay in the game. The team with the most points after two twenty-minute halves wins.

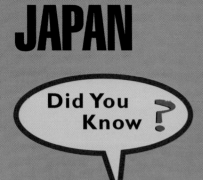

JAPAN

Did You Know?

Golf is a favorite pastime in Japan. Big, crowded cities such as Tokyo have no open space for a golf course, so people go to indoor **driving ranges**. Driving ranges can be three stories high, and at some ranges, more than a hundred golfers can play at the same time!

Baseball is very popular in Japan. There are over 1,500 Little League baseball teams for boys from ages nine to thirteen. The Japanese believe that hard work, politeness, and team spirit are more important than winning a game. No one ever argues with a referee, and fans are sure to applaud both teams at a game.

Japanese martial arts have become popular worldwide. They were first practiced by **Samurai** (SA-muh-rye) as training for battle. These fighting and self-defense techniques later became modern martial arts such as karate, judo, and kendo.

Japanese children like to play nonsports games, too, such as *go*, which is a board game. Many children also play electronic pinball games called *pachinko* (pah-CHING-ko), as well as computer games. In schoolyards, children play traditional games, such as hopscotch and jump rope.

Sumo Wrestling

The ancient art of sumo wrestling is still popular with Japanese **spectators**. A sumo match is full of **rituals**. At the start of a match, wrestlers bow, clap their hands, stomp their feet, and throw salt over their shoulders. The heaviest sumo wrestler on record weighed 496 pounds (225 kilograms)!

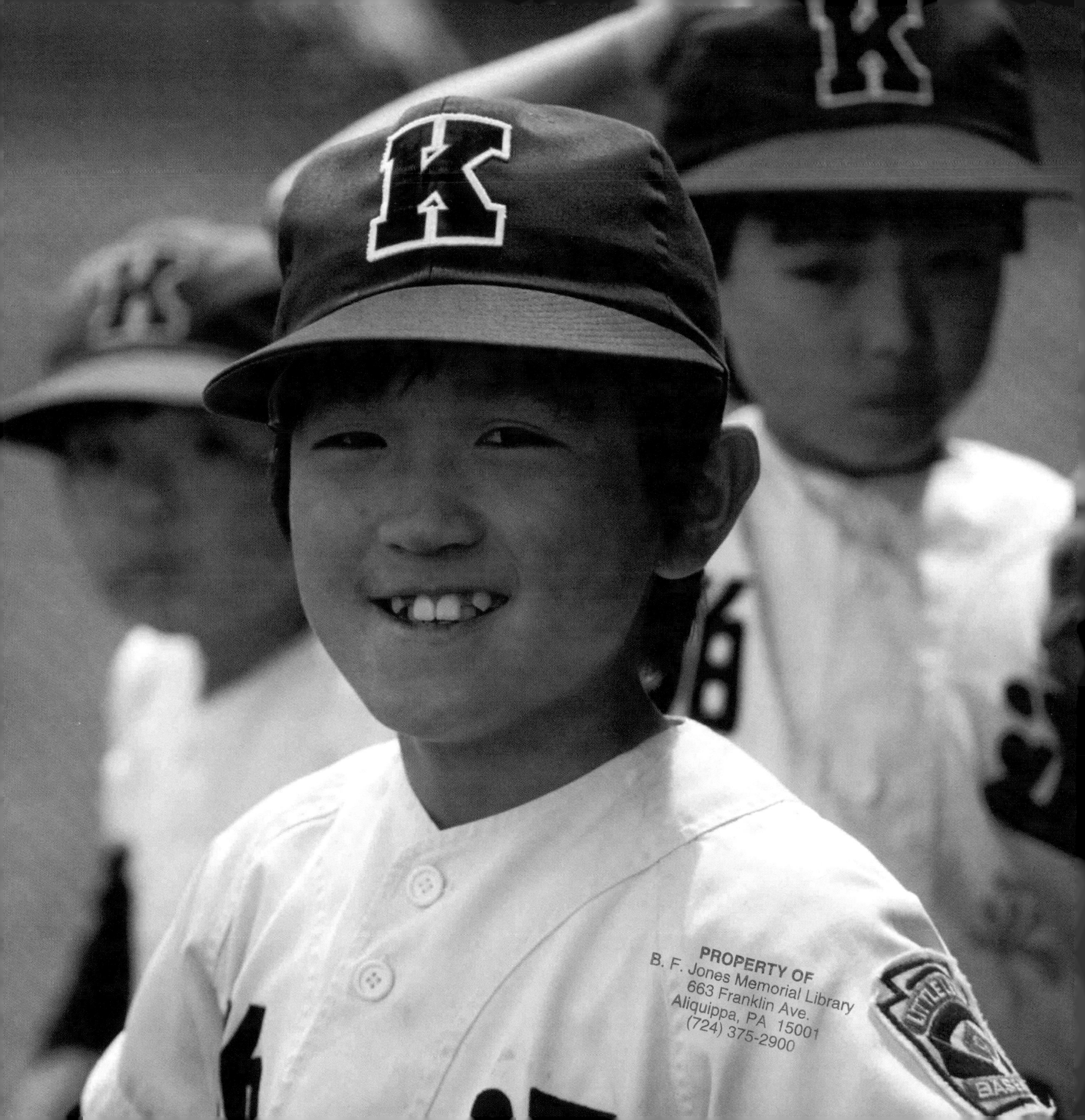

How to play
Ishikeri

Different forms of hopscotch are popular throughout the world. Here is one from Japan.

You will need:
- **two or more players**
- **chalk to mark the court on concrete or a stick to mark the court on dirt**
- **one stone for each player**

❶ Copy the diagram (right) onto your playing area. Draw each space large enough to step in. Number the spaces as shown.

❷ The first player drops a stone in the space numbered 1. The player jumps over space 1 and hops through the court on one foot, hopping once in each space from 2 to 7. The player hops into spaces 8 and 9 at the same time with one foot in each space. The player hops again in spaces 8 and 9 to turn around.

❸ The player then hops back down the court on one foot to space 2.

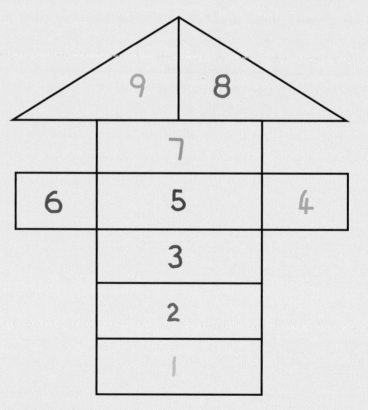

4 At space 2, while balancing on one foot, the player picks up the stone dropped in space 1. Then the player hops in space 1 and leaves the court.

5 Each player, in turn, drops a stone in space 1 and hops through the court. The next round of turns begins with the first player dropping a stone in space 2.

6 A player's turn ends for any of the following reasons:

- if the player's stone does not land in the correct space
- if the stone or the player's foot touches a line
- if the player lands in any space with both feet
- if any part of the player's body, except the foot, touches the ground
- if the player hops in a space that has a stone in it

7 When a player loses a turn, his or her stone remains in the space where it was dropped, and all players must hop over that space.

8 The winner is the first player to have hopped through the court after dropping his or her stone in every numbered space.

MEXICO

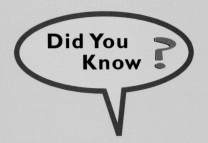

Did You Know?

Mexico City has the biggest bullfighting ring in the world. It seats 55,000 people.

Ulama (ooh-LAH-mah) is a ball game that is still played in Mexico today. It resembles a game that was played by the **Aztecs** more than four hundred years ago.

Mexicans have played ball for more than three thousand years. As long ago as 1600 B.C., ancient people of Mexico called the Olmec (OHL-meck) made the first rubber balls. They mixed sap from a rubber tree with juice from a morning glory vine so the rubber would not become brittle, and the ball would last longer. When Spanish explorers first saw a bouncing rubber ball, they thought it was magic. The ruins of at least six hundred ball courts have been found in Mexico.

Today, Mexican children play basketball, volleyball, baseball, and tennis. Soccer, the most popular sport, is played nearly everywhere. Every town, small or large, has its own team. The biggest soccer matches are played in Mexico City's Aztec Stadium. Right next to Aztec Stadium is Mexico City's bullring. Bullfighting is a very popular spectator sport. In some parts of Mexico, children participate in festive rodeos called *charreadas* (chahr-ray-AH-dahs). Cowboys and cowgirls compete in roping, branding, and sidesaddle and bareback riding contests.

How to play in a **Mexican Maze**

You will need:
- two or more players
- large rocks or objects to mark the path
- rubber ball, about as big as a softball
- stopwatch

❶ To mark the path of the maze, place one rock or object at the starting point, one at the finishing point, and others wherever the path is not clear. The path can go around trees, over stumps, or even through objects on a playground. You can make the maze as difficult or as easy as you want.

❷ Each player takes a turn kicking the ball through the maze, using only his or her feet. Players are not allowed to touch the ball with their hands.

❸ A player's turn begins when the person with the stopwatch says "Go!"

❹ The person with the stopwatch times each player. The player who finishes the maze the fastest is the winner.

How to make a
Rubber Band Ball

You will need:
- **lots of colorful rubber bands**

❶ Scrunch about ten rubber bands into a ball.

❷ Wrap this core of rubber bands with more rubber bands to hold it together. As you add rubber bands, you will see a ball forming.

❸ Add as many rubber bands as you want to get the right ball size. Or stop when you run out of rubber bands!

RUSSIA

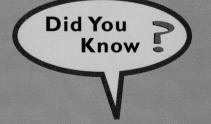

Did You Know ?

Tetris, which is one of the most popular computer games in the world, was invented by a Russian computer programmer named Alexey Pajitnov.

Ice hockey is the national sport of Russia. It is also the fastest team sport in the world. Skaters use curved sticks to shoot and pass around a small **puck** on an indoor ice rink or a frozen lake. A hockey puck can reach speeds of about 130 miles (209 km) per hour! Russian ice hockey teams have won more than twenty world championships and many Olympic medals.

Some Russians enjoy swimming so much they will even swim outdoors during the winter. When the Muscva (mahs-KVA) River freezes, members of the Polar Bear Club of Moscow jog to the shore, cut a hole in the ice, rub their bodies with snow, and jump into the cold water.

In Russia, almost everyone plays chess, and chess champions in Russia are as famous as professional athletes in other countries. Because playing chess takes a lot of brain power, children train their minds by playing chess in school.

Russian Gymnastics

Russia has won many gold medals in gymnastics at the Olympics. Children in Russia start training to be gymnasts at a very young age. One of the most famous and well-loved Russian gymnastic stars is Olga Korbut, who won two gold medals and one silver medal at the 1972 Winter Olympics.

How to do a **Headstand**

Like many sports, gymnastics takes training.
The more you practice, the better you will get at it.

❶ Start next to a wall so you can lean against it. Put a pillow or a cushion where your head will be. Place your head and hands in a triangle position with your head on the pillow and the palms of your hands flat on the floor.

❷ Place your left knee on your left elbow. Then place your right knee on your right elbow. Keep your elbows very still as you slowly lift your toes off the floor. Stay in this position until you get your balance.

3 Lift your knees off your elbows, pushing hard against the floor with your hands. Use the muscles in your back to lift your legs.

4 Straighten your knees and push your toes up toward the ceiling.

5 Practice staying in a headstand for about twenty seconds.

6 To get down, carefully bend your legs and lower them, one at a time.

7 When you can easily do a headstand against the wall, try one away from the wall.

SOUTH AFRICA

Did You Know ❓

In South Africa, games that are not championship games are called "friendlies."

"Draughts" is the name for checkers in South Africa.

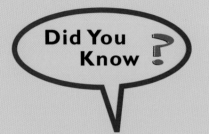

One of the popular sports in South Africa is rugby. Rugby is a fast-paced sport — the action never stops! Many rugby teams in South Africa have animal names, such as the Cheetahs, the Lions, the Elephants, the Leopards, the Pumas, the Sharks, and the Springboks.

In South African cities, children play soccer, tennis, basketball, and junior cricket. In rural or tribal areas, guarding cattle is a common chore for children and an important job for the well-being of whole communities. Native South African tribal societies depend on cattle herding for their livelihoods. In these areas, traditional games are passed down from one generation to the next. Some of these games teach young boys how to be good shepherds.

Xhosa (KOH-sah) and Zulu boys learn the game of stick fighting at the age of five or six. Stick fighting helps them learn how to protect grazing areas from wild animals. Many games use stones to symbolize cattle. The most popular of these games is *moraba-raba*. A version of this game, which was first played seven thousand years ago, is called *mancala*. In Arabic, *mancala* means "transfer."

How to play **Moraba-Raba**

The object of *moraba-raba* is to be the player who ends up with the most stones. The stones represent cows, a traditional symbol of wealth in South Africa.

You will need:

- **two players**
- **forty-eight small stones, pebbles, or seeds**
- **empty egg carton**

❶ To set up the game, place the egg carton between the two players. Fill each hole with four "cows," as shown (below).

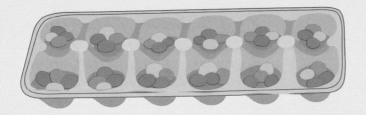

❷ The first player picks up all four cows from one hole on his or her side of the egg carton. Starting with the next hole to the right and moving counterclockwise, the player drops one cow in each hole.

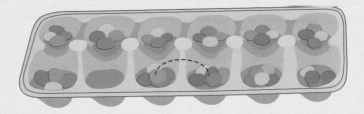

❸ The second player picks up all four cows from a hole on his or her side of the egg carton and drops them in the next four holes, moving counterclockwise. Neither player can win any cows on the first turn.

4 A player can win cows, on any other turn, by dropping the last cow into a hole that has only two or three cows. The player then keeps all the cows from that hole.

5 If a player drops the last cow into a hole that has fewer than two or more than three cows, the player cannot keep the cows, and the next player takes a turn.

6 A player who picks up twelve or more cows from a hole at the start of a turn does not put one in the next hole. The player must skip that hole and start with the hole after it.

7 The game ends when all six holes on one side of the egg carton are empty. The player with the most cows is the winner.

UNITED STATES

Did You Know?

The first skateboards were invented by surfers in California who wanted to practice surfing on land. By attaching wheels to pieces of wood, they were able to "surf" the streets and sidewalks.

The United States is one of the few countries where soccer is not the most popular sport. In most other countries, soccer is called "football." American football is more like rugby than soccer. In the United States, football is a unique national sport.

From March to October, baseball is America's national pastime, and basketball was invented in the United States. In 1891, James Naismith, who was a physical education teacher in Springfield, Massachusetts, came up with a new game that could be played indoors during the winter. He nailed peach baskets to the balcony of a gymnasium and had his students take turns throwing a soccer ball into the baskets for points. Today, basketball is played all over the world.

"Extreme" sports, such as skateboarding, snowboarding, mountain biking, and in-line skating, were **pioneered** by American children and teenagers. Athletes in these sports perform exciting tricks, such as skating down stair railings or flipping skateboards off ramps and spinning in the air.

As in many other countries, some of the games in America are passed down from one generation to the next. Variations of games such as jacks, marbles, and jump rope are found all over the world.

How to play **Marbles**

Marbles is a timeless childhood game in the United States and in many other countries around the world. Children collect marbles and value them for their many sizes and colors.

You will need:
- **two or more players**
- **chalk or stick**
- **marbles, about five for each player**

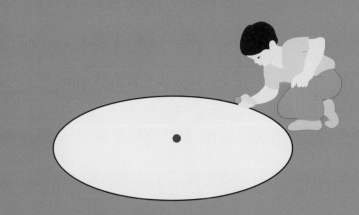

1 Using chalk to draw on pavement or a stick to draw in the dirt, make a circle about 3 feet (1 m) across.

2 One player places a marble in the center of the circle. The other players put their marbles on the ground at the outside edge of the circle and take turns trying to knock the marble out of the circle.

3 A player uses his or her fingers to thump or flick a marble toward the marble in the circle. If the player knocks the marble out of the circle, he or she keeps the marble. If the player is not successful, the next player takes a turn.

4 If a player's marble does not land in the circle, he or she must put it in the circle before the next player shoots.

5 If one player knocks another player's marble out of the circle and captures it, the player who lost the marble must put another one in the circle. The game continues until all of the marbles are captured.

Marbles can be played "for fair," which means that all the marbles are given back to their owners when the game is over, or "for keeps," which means that the winner gets to keep the marbles he or she has captured.

How to play **Twenty-One**

The object of this game is to be the first player to score twenty-one points.

You will need:

- **two players**
- **chalk**
- **basketball hoop**
- **basketball**

1 Draw a line about 15 feet (5 m) in front of the basketball hoop.

2 One player stands under the basket. The other player shoots the ball from behind the line. If the shooter makes a basket, he or she scores two points.

3 A player continues to shoot until he or she misses the basket. Then the other player dribbles the ball to the basket and shoots a **layup**. If the ball goes into the basket, the player scores one point and takes a turn at the shooting line. Otherwise, the player loses his or her turn.

4 The first player to score exactly twenty-one points is the winner. A score over twenty-one does not count, so a player with twenty points does not want to shoot from the two-point line.

A layup scores 1 point.

A basket thrown from the line scores 2 points.

Glossary

Aborigines: the earliest inhabitants of Australia

accuracy: correctness

Aztecs: the Native people who ruled the Mexican empire in the 1400s and early 1500s.

barrier reef: a coral reef that follows a shoreline, separated from land by a lagoon

Bedouins: nomadic Arabs who live in the Arabian, Syrian, and North African deserts

colony: a new land or territory settled by people from another country who follow the laws of their home country

cured: prepared or changed through a chemical or physical process

deities: powerful beings that are worshiped as gods

driving ranges: large outdoor or indoor areas that have distance markers, clubs, balls, and tees for practicing golf drives

goalie: the person who protects the goal area in a sport such as soccer or hockey

hieroglyphics: picture writing invented by the ancient Egyptians

layup: a basketball shot made from near the basket, usually by playing the ball off the backboard

luge: an Olympic event in which one or two people ride a small sled down an icy course while lying on their backs

martial art: a type of fighting or self-defense often done as a sport

mascot: a person, animal, or object used as a symbol to bring good luck to a group or a team

nomads: people who move from place to place with no permanent home

pharaoh: a ruler in ancient Egypt

pioneered: started or helped begin a new line of thought or activity

puck: the small hard plastic disk used in ice hockey

rituals: actions that are always done the same way, usually as part of a ceremony

Samurai: warriors in ancient Japan

sinew: a strong fiber or band of tissue that attaches muscle to a bone

spectators: people who watch a sporting event

underdog: in sports, the person or team not expected to win

More Information

Acka Backa BOO! Playground Games from Around the World.
Opal Dunn (Henry Holt)

Games. Around the World (series). Margaret C. Hall (Heinemann Library)

Hopscotch. Games Around the World (series). Elizabeth Dana Jaffe
(Compass Point Books)

Marbles. Games Around the World (series). Elizabeth Dana Jaffe
(Compass Point Books)

Play Around the World. We All Share (series). Patricia Lakin
(Blackbirch Marketing)

Sports. Around the World (series). Margaret C. Hall (Heinemann Library)

Sports from A to Z. Bobbie Kalman and Kate Calder (Crabtree)

Welcome to Germany. Welcome to My Country (series). Nicole Frank
and Richard Lord (Gareth Stevens)

Welcome to India. Welcome to My Country (series). Fiona Conboy
and Sunandini Arora Lal (Gareth Stevens)

Welcome to Mexico. Welcome to My Country (series). Leslie Jermyn
and Fiona Conboy (Gareth Stevens)

Web Sites

Children's Folk Games: Russia
www.geocities.com/athens/styx/6504/russianhome.html

Kids Web Japan: Sports
www.jinjapan.org/kidsweb/japan/e.html

Tales from the Billabong: Billabong Games
www.fraynework.com.au/story/games/

What is Capoeira?
http://www.capoeirasj.com/whatis/

Index